About This Resource

Why is this topic important?

In the work world, there are many moments when people should speak up but are afraid to do so and, instead, suffer in silence. As a result, valuable input is not heard. Sometimes people are not afraid to speak up, but when they do, they show little tact and cause others to be defensive. This training session will help both people who are reluctant to speak up and those who do so with little tact.

What can you achieve with this resource?

This is a guide for the person who wishes to facilitate a training program that motivates individuals to be direct, yet tactful, about their opinions, ideas, and needs. It helps participants to be assertive when appropriate without putting others on the defensive. Participants learn to speak clearly, forcefully, and respectfully.

Although brief, the program is not a leader-centered presentation or merely an hour of group discussion. Instead, participants are engaged in short activities that heighten their awareness of their current attitudes and behaviors, inspire them to adopt new ones, and provide them with concrete suggestions that can be used immediately back on the job.

How is this resource organized?

The training program can be conducted in one hour (the length can be extended with a more leisurely pace) without making concessions to the extra time that participatory training sessions usually require. It features "active training" techniques in which lecturing is minimized and learning activity is maximized. The 60-minute format allows the facilitator to provide effective training in a brief time period. As a result, busy employees can attend a training session without disrupting their work day. The active training techniques used in this program are designed to increase participation, enliven learning, deepen retention, and encourage application.

The program can be conducted with as few as four participants and yet also functions well for a larger group. Participants can be drawn from different parts of an organization or be members of an intact team.

About Pfeiffer

Pfeiffer serves the professional development and hands-on resource needs of training and human resource practitioners and gives them products to do their jobs better. We deliver proven ideas and solutions from experts in HR development and HR management, and we offer effective and customizable tools to improve workplace performance. From novice to seasoned professional, Pfeiffer is the source you can trust to make yourself and your organization more successful.

Essential Knowledge Pfeiffer produces insightful, practical, and comprehensive materials on topics that matter the most to training and HR professionals. Our Essential Knowledge resources translate the expertise of seasoned professionals into practical, how-to guidance on critical workplace issues and problems. These resources are supported by case studies, worksheets, and job aids and are frequently supplemented with CD-ROMs, websites, and other means of making the content easier to read, understand, and use.

Essential Tools Pfeiffer's Essential Tools resources save time and expense by offering proven, ready-to-use materials—including exercises, activities, games, instruments, and assessments—for use during a training or team-learning event. These resources are frequently offered in looseleaf or CD-ROM format to facilitate copying and customization of the material.

Pfeiffer also recognizes the remarkable power of new technologies in expanding the reach and effectiveness of training. While e-hype has often created whizbang solutions in search of a problem, we are dedicated to bringing convenience and enhancements to proven training solutions. All our e-tools comply with rigorous functionality standards. The most appropriate technology wrapped around essential content yields the perfect solution for today's on-the-go trainers and human resource professionals.

Essential resources for training and HR professionals

Other 60-Minute Active Training Series Titles

The 60-Minute Active Training Series

HOW TO SPEAK UP WITHOUT PUTTING OTHERS DOWN

LEADER'S GUIDE

Mel Silberman and Freda Hansburg

Published by Pfeiffer
An Imprint of Wiley
989 Market Street, San Francisco, CA 94103-1741   www.pfeiffer.com

For additional copies/bulk purchases of this book in the U.S. please contact 800-274-4434.

Pfeiffer books and products are available through most bookstores. To contact Pfeiffer directly call our Customer Care Department within the U.S. at 800-274-4434, outside the U.S. at 317-572-3985 or fax 317-572-4002 or www.pfeiffer.com.

Pfeiffer also publishes its books in a variety of electronic formats. Some content that appears in print may not be available in electronic books.

ISBN: 0-7879-7355-6

Acquiring Editor: Martin Delahoussaye

Director of Development: Kathleen Dolan Davies

Developmental Editor: Susan Rachmeler

Editor: Rebecca Taff

Senior Production Editor: Dawn Kilgore

Manufacturing Supervisor: Becky Carreno

Interior Design: Erin Zeltner

Printed in the United States of America

Printing 10 9 8 7 6 5 4 3 2 1

CONTENTS

Getting the Most from This Resource

In today's organizations, more work is done by fewer people, the pace is fast, and immediate results are expected. As a result, a classroom-delivered training program lasting several hours, if not days, is a luxury not always affordable.

One solution is to replace classroom instruction with self-directed e-learning. While this approach is very helpful, it is not the only option. Briefer classroom training also makes sense . . . if the session is highly focused and the pace is accelerated.

You can introduce "60-minute" training by finding a convenient time for a group to assemble. It may be during lunch (as in a "lunch and learn" format), at the beginning or end of the work day, or at any time when a break from "business as usual" may be welcomed. Moreover, the training can be worthwhile with a group as small as four participants. The program can be delivered to much larger groups, as well.

This 60-minute program utilizes a training approach described in the book *Active Training* (Silberman, 1998). The goals of active training are

- To Increase Participation

- To Enliven Learning

- To Deepen Retention

- To Encourage Application

An active approach to training is based on the idea that it's not what *we tell* participants that counts; it's what *they take away*. Learning is not an automatic consequence of pouring information into another person's head. It requires the learner's own mental involvement and doing. Therefore, lecturing should be minimized and learning activity should be maximized.

To increase the chances that participants *take away* a lot, even in a short period of time, this 60-minute active training program has been designed with five key ingredients in mind.

1. Moderate Level of Content

This training session concentrates on critical learning areas—those elements of the subject that provide the essential basis on which to build later. In designing training sessions, the tendency too often is to cover the waterfront by throwing in everything possible about a given subject. After all, you only get one shot at these participants, so you'd better make sure you have covered it all. You may fail to realize, however, that participants will forget far more than they will ever learn. The best approach is to be selective, choosing the "need to know" before the "nice to know." Training sessions that promote active learning have a lean curriculum.

2. Variety of Learning Methods

This training series employs an assortment of learning methods from *101 Ways to Make Training Active,* 2nd ed. (Silberman, 2005). They include self-assessment scales, experiential exercises, small group discussion, role play, and lecturettes. A variety of training approaches keeps interest alive and can help minimize the downtimes when energy levels are low. Another and even more important argument for variety is that adults learn in different ways. Using different learning approaches is likely to be more effective than a single approach that may work for some but not for others.

3. Opportunities for Group Participation

This training session promotes active involvement of participants by utilizing interactive whole group formats, pair discussion/activity, and small group activities. Group participation has advantages in any training session. Involving the group moves training from the passive to the active. Group activity engages participants in the learning process and makes them working partners with the trainer.

4. Utilization of Participants' Experience

Each participant in a training program brings relevant experiences to the session. Some of these experiences will be directly applicable; others may involve analogies from previous jobs or situations. In either case, much of the learning in this training session comes from one's peers.

5. Encouragement of "Back on the Job" Application

At the conclusion of any training session, participants will naturally ask "Now what?" The success of this training session is really measured by how that question is answered—that is, how what has been learned in the session is transferred to the job. Therefore, the training session ends with "experiments in change" . . . activities that the participants can undertake to apply back on the job.

All the essential information you need to conduct this training session follows. Included are an overview of the program and statement of objectives, an outline to view the program at a glance, step-by-step program directions, and general tips for successful facilitation. Prior to conducting the session, you should carefully read through this Leader's Guide and the accompanying Participant's Workbook.

Sixty minutes is a short period of time to conduct effective training. You might wonder how you can do justice to the topic in such a brief period. Our solution is to provide participants with a short article (included in the Participant's Workbook) they can read after the session to provide more detailed information and guidance. Moreover, the inclusion of active training elements can be time-consuming as well. However, if the training elements are well-chosen, a short program can have a substantial impact. Have confidence that our selection of methods will provide maximum impact in a minimum amount of time.

As you prepare yourself to conduct this program, we encourage you to contact us if you have any questions!

Keep 'em active,

Mel Silberman and Freda Hansburg
Active Training
303 Sayre Drive
Princeton, NJ 08540
800–924–8157
mel@activetraining.com
freda@activetraining.com

Visit us on the web at www.activetraining.com

About This Training Program

In the work world, there are many moments when people should speak up but are afraid to do so and, instead, suffer in silence. Sometimes, people are not afraid to speak up, but when they do, they show little tact and cause others to be defensive. This training session will help both people who are reluctant to speak up and those who do so with little tact.

At work, we need to express our opinions and our needs. Our opinions provide valuable input, feedback, and advice, but if we hold them back, no one will benefit. And if we express them in a manner that makes others defensive, no one will listen to their value.

In order to be effective, at work and elsewhere, we must also have limits and establish those limits. If a person tries to be all things to all people, he or she will wind up disappointing others. We also must be straightforward with our needs. Hinting at what we need from others only leads to disappointment and frustration. Once that happens, we often become angry with others and lose the calm and confidence we need to be at our best. People who are successful at asserting their needs are able to remain calm and confident, even when others try to provoke them and push their emotional buttons. They know how to stay focused on what they want to accomplish, how to express their needs directly, and how to respond effectively when others put on the heat.

Group Size

This program can be conducted with as few as four participants and with as many participants as you like.

Training Objectives

Participants will have the opportunity:

- To discuss the benefits of speaking up

- To assess their assertion skills

- To identify work situations in which speaking up is essential

- To practice assertiveness in difficult situations

- To select "experiments in change" at work

Activity	Time	Participant Workbook Page
1. Welcome *A brief review of training objectives*	2 min.	1
2. Polling the Group *A quick survey about speaking up*	5 min.	
3. Self-Assessment *An opportunity for participants to assess their assertive skills*	5 min.	2
4. Thinking About Assertiveness *An exercise that teaches how to contribute to a team's success*	10 min.	3
5. Coaching Tips *A nonthreatening way to role play*	15 min.	4
6. Practicing Assertiveness *Skill development in pairs*	15 min.	5
7. Experiments in Change *Ways to apply the training*	5 min.	6
8. Bumper Stickers *A closing exercise*	3 min.	7
9. Follow-Up Reading		8 through 15

1. Welcome

(*Time:* 2 minutes; *Materials:* Workbook p. 1)

⟹ Welcome participants, summarize the "About this brief training session" description and refer them to the objectives of the session on page 1 of their workbooks:

- To discuss the benefits of speaking up
- To assess their assertion skills
- To identify work situations in which speaking up is essential
- To practice assertiveness in difficult situations
- To select "experiments in change" at work

2. Polling the Group

(*Time:* 5 minutes)

⟹ Ask the group the questions below. Request a show of hands for each question. Record the number of hands up for each question. Move the polling along quickly.

- *How many of you have ever withheld your misgivings about how a project, event, or procedure is going?*
- *How many of you have ever agreed to things you really did not support?*
- *How many of you have ever allowed other people to make requests on your time and energy that impede your job performance?*
- *How many of you have ever excused behavior that should not have been tolerated?*

⟹ When you have completed the polling, revisit some of the questions and ask participants to share quick examples.

3. Self-Assessment

(*Time:* 5 minutes; *Materials:* Workbook p. 2)

⟹ Invite participants to complete the brief assessment on page 2.

⟹ Pair up participants and ask them to share their ratings with their partners.

⟹ Reconvene the group and request that a few people share which abilities are a challenge for them. Try to have them identify work-related examples.

4. Thinking About Assertiveness

(*Time:* 10 minutes; *Materials:* Workbook p. 3)

⟹ Re-form participants into pairs. Refer them to page 3, Thinking About Assertiveness, and ask them to take five minutes to discuss with their partners their responses to the questions below:

- *When is it difficult to speak freely about your opinions and needs?*

- *Why is it important to assert your opinions and needs?*

- *How can you avoid putting others down or making them upset with you when you "speak up"?*

⟹ Hold an open discussion of the above questions. To keep control of your time, ask for two or three volunteers for each question. Bring in these key points:

- People often censor what they really think and feel because of "office gossip," fear of not adhering to the "party line," or wanting to be seen as a "team player."

- No one has to express everything that's on his or her mind, but it is helpful to the organization's success if people feel free to provide input, even if it may be unpopular.

- The key is to be calm and confident by slowing yourself down, speaking briefly and nondefensively, and staying focused on what you want to achieve (rather than discrediting others). It helps to use "I" rather than "you," to avoid words like "always" and "never," and not to impute another's motives.

5. Coaching Tips

(*Time:* 15 minutes; *Materials:* Workbook p. 4)

⇒ Refer to page 4, Coaching Tips, and give participants time to review it. Invite comments and questions.

⇒ Ask for two or three participants to share a work situation in which they have had difficulty asserting their needs. Choose one situation. Interview the participant to help him or her be as clear as possible on what is wanted from the other person.

⇒ Next, ask the designated participant to portray the other person in the situation. Offer to take the role of the person you have selected. In essence, you are reversing roles. Reenact a recent situation. Obtain as much information as possible in order to be able to portray the person realistically.

⇒ Before beginning the role play, ask the audience to consult the coaching tips on page 4 and then give you advice on how to start off on the right foot. Listen to a few proposals. Act out those ideas that are consistent with someone with good assertive skills. Then stop.

⇒ Now encourage the "other person" to give you a hard time. Again ask for advice from the audience. Employ suggestions that help you to remain calm, confident, and persistent.

6. Practicing Assertiveness

(*Time:* 15 minutes; *Materials:* Workbook p. 5)

⇒ Ask each participant to complete page 5, Practicing Assertiveness.

⇒ Reconvene pairs. Request that each person in the pair take a turn describing a situation in which he or she would like to be more assertive. Request that each partner discuss first exactly what he or she wants in the situation. Then have the person enlist the partner to be the "other person." Give pairs the opportunity to rehearse how they might deal more assertively with the situation. Remind participants:

- *Take a deep breath, slow yourself down, and talk just enough to express your wishes.*

- *Don't become defensive or caught up in power struggles or blow your cool.*

- *When necessary, repeat yourself like a "broken record" in order to stand your ground.*

- *When you hear objections, use phrases like: "That may be," "We see it differently," "That's true and. . .," "I realize how important this is to you, and . . . ."*

- *Give brief, nonapologetic explanations for your position.*

How to Speak Up Without Putting Others Down: Leader's Guide

7. Try It: Experiments in Change

(*Time:* 5 minutes; *Materials:* Workbook p. 6)

⟹ Ask participants to look over the choices found on page 6, Experiments in Change, and select at least one they would like to undertake in the next week.

⟹ Invite participants to share their choices with their partners.

⟹ Briefly survey the choices made by the entire group.

8. Bumper Stickers

(*Time:* 3 minutes; *Materials:* Workbook p. 7)

⟹ Ask participants to turn to page 7, Bumper Sticker, in their workbooks.

⟹ Invite participants to create a "bumper sticker" that advertises or promotes a key thought or piece of advice they will keep in mind to guide them in the future as they apply this training lesson (for example: "Stay calm and confident").

⟹ After two minutes, invite willing participants to display their bumper stickers or merely to shout out the slogan. Applaud the results.

9. Follow-Up Reading

⟹ Encourage participants to read Speaking Up Without Putting Others Down on pages 8 to 15 outside of the session.

As you conduct this 60-minute training session, bear in mind that active training is especially successful if you do a good job as facilitator. Following are several tips to ensure your success.

Pre-Planning

Your participants will get the most out of this training experience if you follow these general recommendations:

- If possible, have participants do something before they come to the session. For example, provide the article for follow-up reading that accompanies this session to participants for pre-reading instead. Or give participants some questions to think about before the session.

- Customize some of the forms provided for this session so that they reflect as closely as possible the work environment of the participants and the language they would find user-friendly.

- Try to find your own words and illustrate key points with your own examples and personal stories. In addition, alter the sequence of activities when you feel it would be helpful to you in a particular situation. Also, skip details that don't add value for you or the group you are training.

- Encourage participants to identify and discuss their own work situations throughout the session. However, assure them that all conversations are private and confidential.

- Skill practice is a vital part of this program. Role-playing formats are used in the design, such as skits, participant-coached role plays demonstrated by the facilitator, and simultaneous role playing in pairs. Adjust these formats to your needs and the comfort level of your participants.

- As mentioned before, the session ends with "experiments in change" . . . suggested back-on-the-job activities to reinforce your training efforts. Think in advance how you will motivate participants to undertake an experiment in change by offering your availability as a coach or mentor.

Setup

Arrange the physical environment of your 60-minute session to maximize participation and involvement. To accomplish this, use any of the following arrangements:

1. U Shape

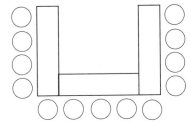

This is an all-purpose setup for up to eighteen participants (three sides of six). (More participants create a setup in which some participants are either too far from you or from each other.) The participants have a reading/writing surface, see you and/or a visual medium easily, and are in face-to-face contact with one another. It's also easy to pair up participants. The arrangement is ideal for distributing handouts quickly to participants since you can enter the U and walk to different points with sets of materials. Be sure there is enough perimeter space in the room so that subgroups of three or more participants can pull back from the tables and face each other.

2. Team Style

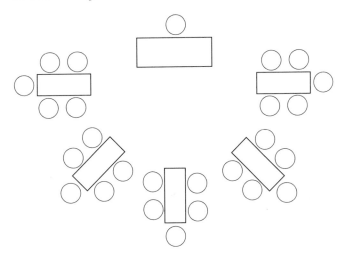

Grouping circular or oblong tables around the classroom enables you to promote team interaction. If you leave the mouth of each table empty, participants can easily see you in the front of the room without having to turn their chairs around. The ideal team table seats six participants. You then can have a subgroup of six, two trios, or three pairs.

3. Conference Table

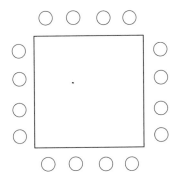

It's best if the table is relatively circular or square. This arrangement minimizes the importance of the leader and maximizes the importance of the group. A rectangular or oval table often creates a sense of formality if you are "at the head of the table," so if you have this type of table, sit in the middle of a wider side. A conference table arrangement works well for pair activity. You need to have perimeter space to create subgroups of three or more.

Facilitating Discussion

Your role during a group discussion is to facilitate the flow of comments from participants. Although it is not necessary to interject after each participant speaks, periodically assisting the group with their contributions can be helpful. Here are some actions to consider:

1. *Paraphrase* what someone has said so that the participant feels understood and the other participants can hear a concise summary of what's been said.

2. *Check your understanding* against the words of a participant or ask a participant to clarify what he or she is saying.

3. *Compliment* an interesting or insightful comment.

4. *Elaborate* on a participant's contribution to the discussion with examples or suggest a new way to view the problem.

5. *Energize* a discussion by quickening the pace, using humor, or, if necessary, prodding the group for more contributions.

6. *Pull together* ideas, showing their relationship to each other.

Facilitating Experiential Activities

When facilitating experiential activities, here are steps to take to be successful:

1. *Explain your objectives.* Participants like to know what is going to happen and why.

2. *Sell the benefits.* Explain why you are doing the activity and share how the activity connects with the other activities before it.

3. *Speak slowly and/or provide visual backup when giving directions.* Make sure the instructions are understandable.

4. *Demonstrate the activity.* If the directions are complicated, let the participants see it in action before they do it.

5. *Divide participants into subgroups before giving further directions.* If you don't, participants may forget the instructions while the groups are being formed.

6. *Inform participants how much time they have.* State the time allotted for the entire activity and then announce periodically how much time remains.

Saving Time

In a 60-minute session, time is at a premium. It's crucial that no time be wasted. Here are things you can do to avoid wasting time:

1. *Start on time.* This act sends a message to latecomers that you're serious. In the event that all of the participants are not yet in the room, begin the class, if you wish, with a discussion or filler activity for which complete attendance is not necessary.

2. *Give clear instructions.* Do not start an activity when participants are confused about what to do. If the directions are complicated, put them in writing.

3. *Prepare visual information ahead of time.* Don't write lecture points on flip charts or the whiteboard while participants watch. Have it prerecorded. Also, decide whether recording participant input is really necessary. If so, don't record the discussion verbatim. Use "headlines" to capture what participants are saying.

4. *Don't let discussions drag on and on.* Express the need to move on, but be sure in later discussion to call on those who didn't have a chance to contribute previously. Or begin a discussion by stating a time limit and suggesting how many contributions time will permit.

5. *Obtain volunteers swiftly.* Don't wait endlessly for them to emerge from the class. You can recruit volunteers before the session begins.

Minimizing Problem Behaviors

Using active training techniques tends to minimize the problems that often plague trainers who rely too heavily on lecture and full group discussion. Nonetheless, difficulties such as monopolizing, distracting, and withdrawing still may occur. Below are interventions you can use:

1. *Signal nonverbally.* Make eye contact with or move closer to participants when they hold private conversations, start to fall asleep, or hide from participation. Press your fingers together (unobtrusively) to signal a wordy participant to finish what he or she is saying. Make a "T" sign (time out) with your fingers to stop unwanted behavior.

2. *Listen actively.* When participants monopolize discussion, go off on a tangent, or argue with you, interject with a summary of their views and then ask others to speak. Or acknowledge the value of their viewpoints and/or invite them to discuss their views with you during a break.

3. *Get your ducks in order.* When the same participants speak up in class while others hold back, pose a question or problem and then ask how many people have a response to it. You should see new hands go up. Call on one of them. The same technique may work when trying to obtain volunteers for role playing.

4. *Invoke participation rules.* From time to time, tell participants that you would like to use rules such as:

   • No laughing during role playing

   • Only participants who have not spoken as yet can participate

   • Build on one another's ideas

   • Speak for yourself, not for others

5. *Use good-natured humor.* One way to deflect difficult behavior is to humor participants. Be careful, however, not to be sarcastic or patronizing. Gently protest the harassment (for example, "Enough, enough for one day!"). Humorously put yourself down instead of the participant (for example, "I guess I'm being stubborn, but. . . .").

6. *Don't take personally the difficulties you encounter.* Remember that many problem behaviors have nothing to do with you. Instead, they are due to personal fears and needs or displaced anger toward someone else. See whether you can pick up cues when this is the case and ask whether participants can put aside the conditions affecting their positive involvement in the training session.

Silberman, M. (2005). *101 ways to make training active (2nd ed.).* San Francisco, CA: Pfeiffer.

Silberman, M. (1998). *Active training (2nd ed.).* San Francisco, CA: Pfeiffer.

Mel Silberman and Freda Hansburg are the authors of *PeopleSmart: Developing Your Interpersonal Intelligence* (Berrett-Koehler, 2000) and *Working PeopleSmart: 6 Strategies for Success* (Berrett-Koehler, 2004). They are also the founders of PeopleSmart Products and Services, an Active Training Company (www.activetraining.com and 800–924–8157).

Mel Silberman is known internationally as a pioneer in the areas of interpersonal skills training, active learning, and team facilitation. As a professor of adult and organizational development at Temple University, he has won two awards for his distinguished teaching. Among his numerous publications are

- *Active Training: A Handbook of Techniques, Designs, Case Examples, and Tips* (Pfeiffer, 1998)

- *The Best of Active Training* (Pfeiffer, 2004)

- *101 Ways to Make Training Active, 2nd ed.* (Pfeiffer, 2005)

- *101 Ways to Make Meetings Active* (Pfeiffer, 1999)

He is also editor of *The ASTD Training and Performance Sourcebook* and *The ASTD Team and Organization Development Sourcebook* (Active Training/ASTD, 2003–2005).

Freda Hansburg is a psychologist in private practice, a training consultant, and an executive coach whose recent clients include BMW of North America, Depository Trust and Clearing Corporation, Merck, and Valero Refining. She has contributed to *The Training and Performance Sourcebook* and made presentations about interpersonal intelligence for ASTD and the OD Network. She is the former director of the Technical Assistance Center, a behavioral health consultation and training program at the University of Medicine and Dentistry of New Jersey.

Pfeiffer Publications Guide

This guide is designed to familiarize you with the various types of Pfeiffer publications. The formats section describes the various types of products that we publish; the methodologies section describes the many different ways that content might be provided within a product. We also provide a list of the topic areas in which we publish.

FORMATS

In addition to its extensive book-publishing program, Pfeiffer offers content in an array of formats, from fieldbooks for the practitioner to complete, ready-to-use training packages that support group learning.

FIELDBOOK Designed to provide information and guidance to practitioners in the midst of action. Most fieldbooks are companions to another, sometimes earlier, work, from which its ideas are derived; the fieldbook makes practical what was theoretical in the original text. Fieldbooks can certainly be read from cover to cover. More likely, though, you'll find yourself bouncing around following a particular theme, or dipping in as the mood, and the situation, dictate.

HANDBOOK A contributed volume of work on a single topic, comprising an eclectic mix of ideas, case studies, and best practices sourced by practitioners and experts in the field.

An editor or team of editors usually is appointed to seek out contributors and to evaluate content for relevance to the topic. Think of a handbook not as a ready-to-eat meal, but as a cookbook of ingredients that enables you to create the most fitting experience for the occasion.

RESOURCE Materials designed to support group learning. They come in many forms: a complete, ready-to-use exercise (such as a game); a comprehensive resource on one topic (such as conflict management) containing a variety of methods and approaches; or a collection of like-minded activities (such as icebreakers) on multiple subjects and situations.

TRAINING PACKAGE An entire, ready-to-use learning program that focuses on a particular topic or skill. All packages comprise a guide for the facilitator/trainer and a workbook for the participants. Some packages are supported with additional media—such as video—or learning aids, instruments, or other devices to help participants understand concepts or practice and develop skills.

- *Facilitator/trainer's guide* Contains an introduction to the program, advice on how to organize and facilitate the learning event, and step-by-step instructor notes. The guide also contains copies of presentation materials—handouts, presentations, and overhead designs, for example—used in the program.

- *Participant's workbook* Contains exercises and reading materials that support the learning goal and serves as a valuable reference and support guide for participants in the weeks and months that follow the learning event. Typically, each participant will require his or her own workbook.

ELECTRONIC CD-ROMs and web-based products transform static Pfeiffer content into dynamic, interactive experiences. Designed to take advantage of the searchability, automation, and ease-of-use that technology provides, our e-products bring convenience and immediate accessibility to your workspace.

METHODOLOGIES

CASE STUDY A presentation, in narrative form, of an actual event that has occurred inside an organization. Case studies are not prescriptive, nor are they used to prove a point; they are designed to develop critical analysis and decision-making skills. A case study has a specific time frame, specifies a sequence of events, is narrative in structure, and contains a plot structure—an issue (what should be/have been done?). Use case studies when the goal is to enable participants to apply previously learned theories to the circumstances in the case, decide what is pertinent, identify the real issues, decide what should have been done, and develop a plan of action.

ENERGIZER A short activity that develops readiness for the next session or learning event. Energizers are most commonly used after a break or lunch to stimulate or refocus the group. Many involve some form of physical activity, so they are a useful way to counter post-lunch lethargy. Other uses include transitioning from one topic to another, where "mental" distancing is important.

EXPERIENTIAL LEARNING ACTIVITY (ELA) A facilitator-led intervention that moves participants through the learning cycle from experience to application (also known as a Structured Experience). ELAs are carefully thought-out designs in which there is a definite learning purpose and intended outcome. Each step—everything that participants do during the activity—facilitates the accomplishment of the stated goal. Each ELA includes complete instructions for facilitating the intervention and a clear statement of goals, suggested group size and timing, materials required, an explanation of the process, and, where appropriate, possible variations to the activity. (For more detail on Experiential Learning Activities, see the Introduction to the *Reference Guide to Handbooks and Annuals*, 1999 edition, Pfeiffer, San Francisco.)

GAME A group activity that has the purpose of fostering team spirit and togetherness in addition to the achievement of a pre-stated goal. Usually contrived—undertaking a desert expedition, for example—this type of learning method offers an engaging means for participants to demonstrate and practice business and interpersonal skills. Games are effective for team building and personal development mainly because the goal is subordinate to the process—the means through which participants reach decisions, collaborate, communicate, and generate trust and understanding. Games often engage teams in "friendly" competition.

ICEBREAKER A (usually) short activity designed to help participants overcome initial anxiety in a training session and/or to acquaint the participants with one another. An icebreaker can be a fun activity or can be tied to specific topics or training goals. While a useful tool in itself, the icebreaker comes into its own in situations where tension or resistance exists within a group.

INSTRUMENT A device used to assess, appraise, evaluate, describe, classify, and summarize various aspects of human behavior. The term used to describe an instrument depends primarily on its format and purpose. These terms include survey, questionnaire, inventory, diagnostic, survey, and poll. Some uses of instruments include providing instrumental feedback to group members, studying here-and-now processes or functioning within a group, manipulating group composition, and evaluating outcomes of training and other interventions.

Instruments are popular in the training and HR field because, in general, more growth can occur if an individual is provided with a method for focusing specifically on his or her own behavior. Instruments also are used to obtain information that will serve as a basis for change and to assist in workforce planning efforts.

Paper-and-pencil tests still dominate the instrument landscape with a typical package comprising a facilitator's guide, which offers advice on administering the instrument and interpreting the collected data, and an initial set of instruments. Additional instruments are available separately. Pfeiffer, though, is investing heavily in e-instruments. Electronic instrumentation provides effortless distribution and, for larger groups particularly, offers advantages over paper-and-pencil tests in the time it takes to analyze data and provide feedback.

LECTURETTE A short talk that provides an explanation of a principle, model, or process that is pertinent to the participants' current learning needs. A lecturette is intended to establish a common language bond between the trainer and the participants by providing a mutual frame of reference. Use a lecturette as an introduction to a group activity or event, as an interjection during an event, or as a handout.

MODEL A graphic depiction of a system or process and the relationship among its elements. Models provide a frame of reference and something more tangible, and more easily remembered, than a verbal explanation. They also give participants something to "go on," enabling them to track their own progress as they experience the dynamics, processes, and relationships being depicted in the model.

ROLE PLAY A technique in which people assume a role in a situation/scenario: a customer service rep in an angry-customer exchange, for example. The way in which the role is approached is then discussed and feedback is offered. The role play is often repeated using a different approach and/or incorporating changes made based on feedback received. In other words, role playing is a spontaneous interaction involving realistic behavior under artificial (and safe) conditions.

SIMULATION A methodology for understanding the interrelationships among components of a system or process. Simulations differ from games in that they test or use a model that depicts or mirrors some aspect of reality in form, if not necessarily in content. Learning occurs by studying the effects of change on one or more factors of the model. Simulations are commonly used to test hypotheses about what happens in a system—often referred to as "what if?" analysis—or to examine best-case/worst-case scenarios.

THEORY A presentation of an idea from a conjectural perspective. Theories are useful because they encourage us to examine behavior and phenomena through a different lens.

TOPICS

The twin goals of providing effective and practical solutions for workforce training and organization development and meeting the educational needs of training and human resource professionals shape Pfeiffer's publishing program. Core topics include the following:

Leadership & Management

Communication & Presentation

Coaching & Mentoring

Training & Development

e-Learning

Teams & Collaboration

OD & Strategic Planning

Human Resources

Consulting

What will you find on pfeiffer.com?

- The best in workplace performance solutions for training and HR professionals

- Downloadable training tools, exercises, and content

- Web-exclusive offers

- Training tips, articles, and news

- Seamless on-line ordering

- Author guidelines, information on becoming a Pfeiffer Affiliate, and much more

Discover more at www.pfeiffer.com

Customer Care

Have a question, comment, or suggestion? Contact us! We value your feedback and we want to hear from you.

For questions about this or other Pfeiffer products, you may contact us by:

E-mail: **customer@wiley.com**

Mail: **Customer Care Wiley/Pfeiffer**
10475 Crosspoint Blvd.
Indianapolis, IN 46256

Phone: **(US) 800-274-4434** (Outside the US: 317-572-3985)

Fax: **(US) 800-569-0443** (Outside the US: 317-572-4002)

To order additional copies of this title or to browse other Pfeiffer products, visit us online at **www.pfeiffer.com**.

For **Technical Support** questions call **(800) 274-4434.**

For authors guidelines, log on to www.pfeiffer.com and click on "Resources for Authors."

If you are . . .

A **college bookstore, a professor, an instructor, or work in higher education** and you'd like to place an order or request an exam copy, please contact jbreview@wiley.com.

A **general retail bookseller** and you'd like to establish an account or speak to a local sales representative, contact Melissa Grecco at 201-748-6267 or mgrecco@wiley.com.

An **exclusively on-line bookseller**, contact Amy Blanchard at 530-756-9456 or ablanchard @wiley.com or Jennifer Johnson at 206-568-3883 or jjohnson@wiley.com, both of our Online Sales department.

A **librarian or library representative**, contact John Chambers in our Library Sales department at 201-748-6291 or jchamber@wiley.com.

A **reseller, training company/consultant, or corporate trainer**, contact Charles Regan in our Special Sales department at 201-748-6553 or cregan@wiley.com.

A **specialty retail distributor** (includes specialty gift stores, museum shops, and corporate bulk sales), contact Kim Hendrickson in our Special Sales department at 201-748-6037 or khendric@wiley.com.

Purchasing for the **Federal government**, contact Ron Cunningham in our Special Sales department at 317-572-3053 or rcunning@wiley.com.

Purchasing for a **State or Local government**, contact Charles Regan in our Special Sales department at 201-748-6553 or cregan@wiley.com.